This book belongs to:

_____

Enjoy :)

Anthony Luke Heydorf

8·19·23

To my wife and kids, you are the best!
Anthony

Text and illustration copyright © 2023 by AH Publishing LLC
Rathdrum, Idaho

ISBN 978-17338093-4-4
ISBN 978-17338093-5-1 (e-book)
Library of Congress Control Number: 2023904732

All rights reserved. This book, characters or any thereof may not be reproduced or used in any manner whatsoever without the express written permission of the publisher except for the use of brief quotation marks in a book review.

Printed and bound in China
First printing edition, 2023
AH PUBLISHING LLC
Contact us at wryt2menow@gmail.com

2 Crows and a Pea

By Anthony Luke Hyslop

Illustrations by Inna Stefanova

"Hey, give me that," cried Titus, just as his little brother, grabbed the last cookie.

"You already had some today, and I didn't get as many as you did," hollered Judah.

"Yes, you did!"

"NO, I didn't!"

"What is going on in here, boys?" asked Dad.

"Judah took my cookie, and he won't give it back!" shouted Titus.

"That was mine, I had it first!" yelled Judah.

"Boys, boys, listen up, I don't know who had more than the other, but there is always a solution. Have I ever told you the story of the Two Crows and a Pea?"

"No," they said shaking their heads.

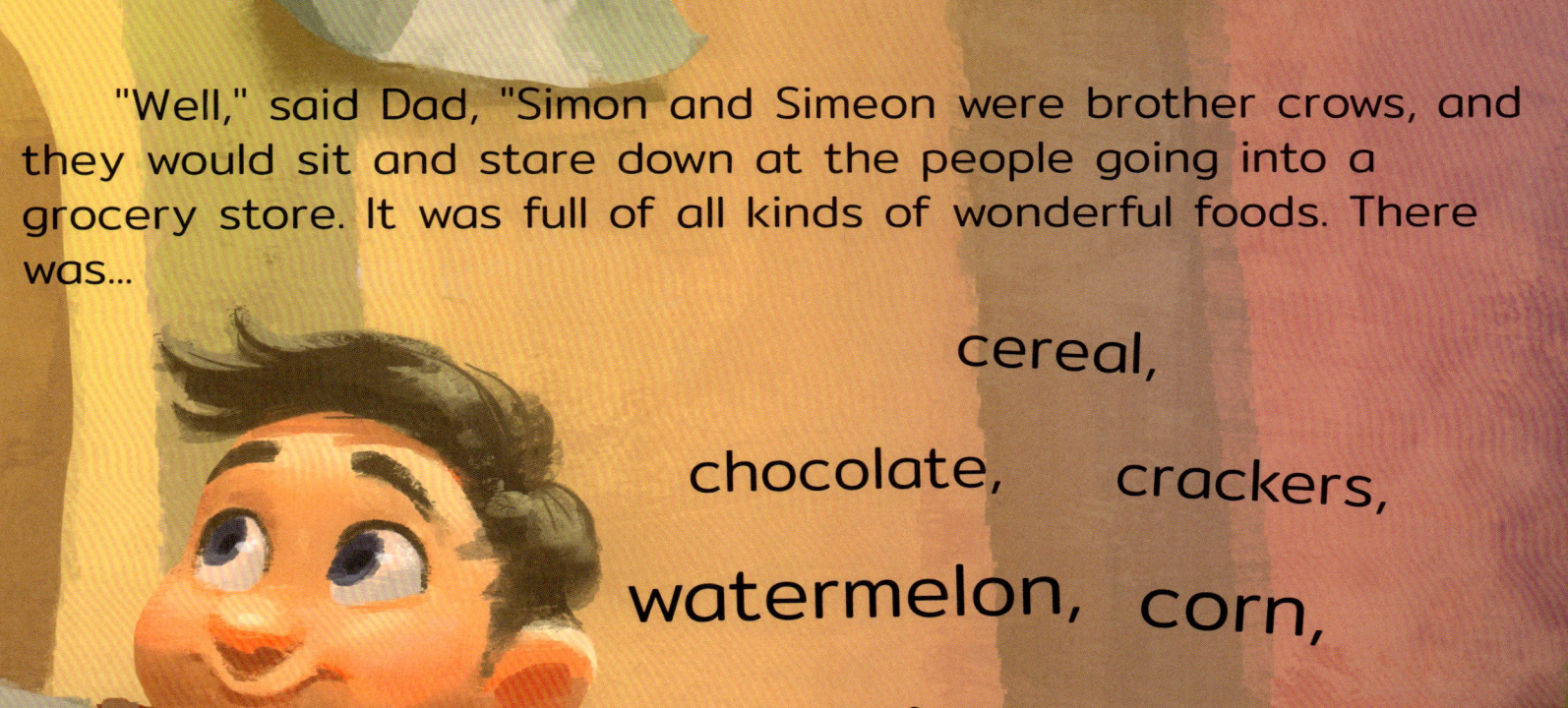

"Well," said Dad, "Simon and Simeon were brother crows, and they would sit and stare down at the people going into a grocery store. It was full of all kinds of wonderful foods. There was...

cereal,

chocolate, crackers,

watermelon, corn,

pizza,

and donuts!

But that day they hadn't eaten, and they were pretty hungry. They sat and waited for any food to drop.

Simon and Simeon listened in...
"Dad, can I eat something?" asked a little boy.
"Sure, how about some fresh peas?"
"Oh, yes!"
The dad grabbed a pea pod and gave it to his son.

"SNAP!"

The little boy cracked the pod, and

"POP!"

the little pea shot up into the air.
Simon heard the snap. Simeon saw the pop.
"Oh boy, oh boy!" cawed Simeon.
"This is it, this is it," thought Simon, nodding his head.

"I am so hungry," said Simeon.
"You might be hungry but I am famished! So I should get to eat it and you wait," cawed Simon.
"I'm younger so I should get it!"

Both brothers squeaked and squawked at each other; as the little pea rolled around during their sibling squabble.

"Simon, last night you said I could have the first bite of the day!" squawked Simeon.

"I did, but then you said that made you feel happy, so then you offered the first bite to me!"

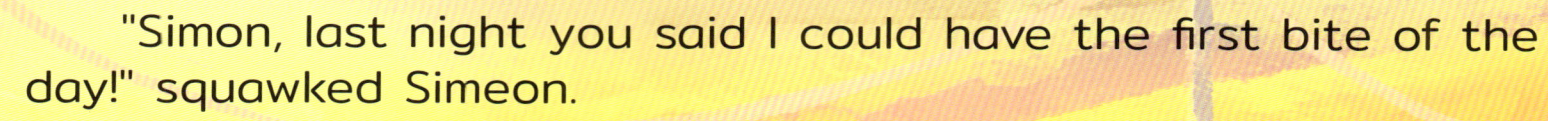

"Just let me have it," hollered Simeon as he picked up the pea.

Well, Simon didn't like that. So he plucked his brother's tail feathers, causing him to drop the pea.

They fought in the air and then on the ground. Trying to do anything they could to hurt the other.

Meanwhile a seagull stood next to their prize, picked up the pea and swallowed it.

After the seagull flew away they noticed their pea was gone!

"I'm sorry for hurting you."
"I'm sorry too little brother," spoke Simon as he put his wing over him.

"So boys, the lesson of this story is... if you can't agree who gets to eat the cookie, or even share it, someone else will come by and enjoy what you both will not. You will be missing the opportunity to be kind and selfless. The joy from sharing from something like this will be gone."

"And that is the story of the 2 Crows and a Pea."

Back story of

2 Crows and a Pea

In 2018, on a Sunday while driving to church with the family, I saw 2 crows along side the road and as we came up on them they flew away. I was in my creative head space at the time, so I thought to myself what would 2 crows be doing together, the title came to me first then the story later. I love incorporating my kids into my stories some how, so I gave this story an Aesop Fable vibe, to teach a moral lesson of sharing, giving, and even the consequences of a fight.

Feb '19, Titus 4, Judah 2

June '22, Titus 8, Judah 6

There are 4 things hidden in plain sight in the illustrations, if you think you found them tag me on Instagram and use the hashtag #2crowsandapea

If you enjoyed reading this book, will you please consider leaving a review on your platform of choice. Reviews help self published authors find more readers like you.

Questions to consider:
- Is it easy or hard for you to share with another?
- Can you think of a time you chose to give up something for someone?
- Has someone shared with you before, how did it make you feel?
- What is something you can think of to share with another? Maybe your possessions, time, or friendship?

Anthony

Anthony Hyslop was born in St. Clair, Michigan in 1986, moved to north Idaho at the age of 7 with his family, was home schooled, and went into concrete flat work, working for his father for the past 19 years. During that time he married his first love, Elizabeth in 2007. They have had 7 children, Clarence, Daphne, Dakota, Kirsten, Titus, Judah, and Caleb, the latter now living with the Lord. They have a black cat named Rocky, and 14 chickens.

Anthony loves to hunt, look for antlers, snorkel, go to the lake with the kids, go to the movies with his wife, create new stories and write poetry from time to time. He believes all good things come from the Lord, and be a good steward of what is given to you.

Facebook: Stories by Anthony Hyslop @ahstories
Instagram: @ahpublishing

Inna Stefanova (Stefahen) is a concept artist and illustrator. Originally Inna is from Russia but now lives in Vilnius, Lithuania, with her beloved husband and a little fluffy cat, Kesha. After her university, she was supposed to be a teacher of the Russian language to foreigners but at some point, she decided not to pursue this career and dive into her real passion, which is painting. As an artist she is self-taught and she doesn't believe in innate talent, she believes that everything that you are truly passionate about is absolutely achievable as long as you stay positive and don't give up trying.

Links on my portfolio:
ArtStation: @stefahen
Instagram: @stefahen

Inna

Look for other titles by this Author:

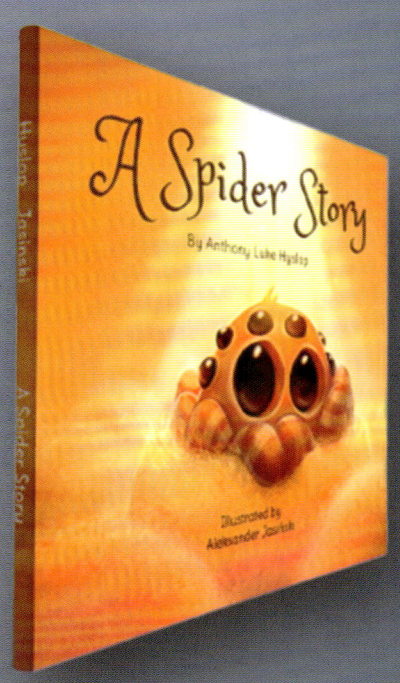

A Spider Story

I could feel some of the eggs opening.
I could feel them moving next to me
and stepping all over me.
Oops! I'm sorry. I never introduced
myself.
I'm Clarence and this is the story
of my very first memories.

A Sci-Fi Christmas

Imagine lying in bed Christmas Eve night,
and being surprised by a visit from Santa
Claus in your neighborhood. "Wait! Who
else is out there?" Find out in this fantastic
tale written in rhyme, in one boy's
eyewitness account of this magical night!

Inna Stefanova's sketches

Would you like to write and illustrate a page?

What do you think Titus and Judah did next? Or continue the story of Simon and Simeon. Use your imagination!

_____

_____

_____

_____

_____

_____

_____

_____

Draw here!